Table of Contents

p. 03	Introduction
p. 04	The History of EBay
p. 05	The Benefits of Being an EBay Powerseller
p. 07	The Workings of EBay
p. 09	Start Selling
p. 11	Seller Registration
p. 17	Listing your Items
p. 24	Writing Descriptions that Sell the Item
p. 27	Including Photos in your EBay Listing
p. 30	Rules for Selling
p. 32	EBay Store Fronts
p. 35	EBay Administrative Services
p. 36	What Sells and What Doesn't Sell
p. 40	Finding Items to Sell
p. 44	Finding a Wholesaler
p. 46	Building a Powerseller Reputation
p. 49	Selling Techniques
p. 52	Selling Issues to Avoid
p. 53	Toolkits for EBay
p. 54	EBay Pitfalls
p. 55	User Agreement
p. 57	Unauthorized Copyright
p. 57	Conclusion

Introduction

Are you interested in earning extra money from the comfort of your own home? There is a saying that one man's junk is another man's treasure! That treasure can be found on eBay. This e-book is all you need to start using eBay to earn that extra money by becoming a powerseller. By applying the information found in this book you will be on your way to becoming a successful eBay seller.

EBay provides you with a simple way to supplement your income, sell items you no longer want or need, liquidate an estate, or sell items from your collection. EBay is a proven e-commerce site on the Internet that specializes in sales using an online auction method. Since eBay appeared on the Internet in 1995 it has consistently generated its own profit and also promoted further success for online sellers and buyers. EBay's proven formula for helping people sell their items works easily and is something that you can learn quickly. EBay's website has everything you need to start your at-home business or simply make a few extra dollars by getting rid of those items around the house that you no longer want.

Once you have decided on a product that you would like to sell on eBay you need to find your market niche. Do your research carefully and then follow the steps on eBay's website to register and begin selling. It's that easy!

Selling on eBay is a great way to start your new business if you're willing to put in the energy and time to be successful. One of the reasons that eBay is an excellent

place to sell your items is because of the large number of people who visit eBay on a daily basis. With such a large volume of customers you are sure to sell any item.
The chapters in this e-book will provide you with step-by-step guidance to show you what you need to do to start selling and learn what it takes to become a powerseller. You will learn how to:

- Register at eBay so that you can sell your items.
- How to create an exciting and eye-catching item description.
- The benefits of selling using eBay.
- What items to sell and what sells fast.
- Where to find items to sell.
- How to build you seller's reputation.
- Tips for selling on eBay.

You are in control of how much money you want to make. And you are in control of when you want to start seeing that profit! Start today to earn extra dollars by using eBay as your selling partner.

The History of EBay

EBay has just celebrated its 10th birthday. It was founded in 1995 by a man named Pierre Omidyar. EBay's original name was "Auction Web" but was changed to "EBay", short for "Echo Bay", which was the name of Omidyar's consulting firm. A main concept of eBay is that it doesn't sell items to people; it simply connects them and allows them to get on with the practice of selling. EBay has created a trusted community for buyers and sellers in a virtual marketplace.

EBay's instant success was amazing. By the end of 1998 there were over 2.1 million registered users and eBay had become the most visited auction site on the Internet. Today there are over 114 million registered users, most of whom are buyers.

EBay continues to lead the online selling market with their innovative buying and selling techniques. The concept of eBay, which is to unite buyers and sellers at one place on the Internet, continues to prove profitable for everyone involved, whether it is a buyer or a seller. EBay is an excellent example of a highly successful e-commerce site that continues to grow on a yearly basis.

The Benefits of Being an EBay Powerseller

Selling on eBay is becoming more and more popular. One of the reasons for this is the many benefits that come with selling online using a secure and reputable company such as eBay. EBay appeals to buyers because:

- They are looking for bargains that they can find in one place, in this case a virtual marketplace.
- They are looking for hard to find items.
- They are looking for items that they collect.

The first benefit of selling at eBay is that you have very little to lose. There are no start-up costs at eBay and this means that you are not risking any of your money to start a new money-making project. You can get started quickly with very little investment. Investment on your part is limited to the products you are selling and the minimal fee that eBay charges you for listing your items.

You can sell on eBay in your spare time. This means that you can keep your full time job and make extra money on the side. You can determine how much or how little time you want to invest in selling items on eBay.

You will be able to work from your own home, from anywhere in the world where you have an Internet connection. There is no need for you to have your own website. EBay does all of the Internet hosting for you. This is perfect for stay-at-home parents who want to earn money while staying home with their children. You can start selling with absolutely no marketing experience.

When you list your sellable items at eBay you can be certain that buyers are coming to you. All you have to do is create an eBay listing for your item that is catchy and makes buyers read it twice. Be accurate and concise when creating the description for your items. More information is better than not enough information. Giving buyers the opportunity to ask you questions about the item you are selling is an important technique that you should use consistently.

Using a virtual marketplace to sell your items means that you don't have to take your sellable items to an auction house or flea market to make extra money. It can be time consuming and exhausting to haul your items back and forth in your attempt to sell them.

EBay is simple and easy to use. Once you sell one or two items you will become more and more confident with the way the selling process works. EBay is designed to make the process of selling your items as easy and uncomplicated as possible while at the same time working in a seamless and successful fashion. Help at eBay is always near at hand so you never have to wait if you require assistance.

There are many other benefits of using eBay to sell items. The key factor is that it all comes down to your personal preferences. You are in control of what you sell and the manner in which you are going to sell it. You are the one who decides how much effort and time you invest in the business of online e-commerce.

The Workings of EBay

EBay works in a very simple manner. There are no hidden secrets for you to learn before you start selling online and there are no hidden costs credited to you. All you have to do is list an item for sale on eBay. The item can be as simple as a watch or as elaborate as your lost uncle's stamp collection. You can either accept bids on your item in an auction format or you can offer buyers the "Buy It Now" option that allows them to buy your item immediately.

Powersellers quickly learn what sells on eBay and what doesn't. When you find an item, or a group of items, that sell well you'll want to learn to utilize your selling techniques as much as possible.

The online auction method is simple to understand.

The opening bidding price begins at a price that you determine for a certain number of days, chosen by you. During this time buyers place bids on your item. At the end of the listing period the highest bidder wins the item.

The "Buy It Now" method of selling simply means that the first buyer who is willing to pay the price you are asking for your item wins the auction.

There are some things that you should know and understand about the selling process at eBay. These important points will be discussed in a later chapter.

EBay provides you with all the tools you need to begin your selling your items immediately. EBay has fine-tuned the art of the online auction by trial and error. They want to ensure your success and have developed a step-by-step formula for you to register, list your items, maintain your eBay account, and make a profit. EBay's step-by-step formula includes:

- Decide what you want to sell and do the appropriate research to become knowledgeable about your item.
- Register at eBay and get a seller's account.
- Accurately and concisely create an eBay "listing" for the item you are selling.

- Receive payment from the buyer after your item sells.

EBay's online virtual marketplace has all the tools you need to sell successfully and make a profit. The simplicity of eBay makes it easy for you sell confidently in a stress-free online atmosphere.

Start Selling

It's easy to start selling at eBay since the process is easy and smooth to understand and implement….and it costs you very little money to get started. One of the most significant things to note about selling on eBay is that there is little financial risk involved to get you started. Most new businesses require large amounts of money to cover start-up costs such as rent and distribution.

There are really only a few things that you need to become a powerseller on eBay:

- products to sell
- a digital camera so that you can take pictures of the items that you're selling an upload them to the eBay website
- a computer
- the enthusiasm to become an eBay powerseller and increase your annual income

You'll want to make sure that you have enough room in your house to accommodate the items that you're going to be selling. You'll need to have room set aside not only to store these items but also a space set aside where you can manage the shipping of these items. If your goal is to be a huge eBay powerseller you might want to eventually find a space to rent so that you can sell your items in large quantities.

There are many sellers on eBay since the process of signing up is so simple. Becoming an eBay powerseller is just one step away from being a seller who sells only the occasional item. Powersellers make multiple sales each month and earn high profits from these sales.

Getting started selling at eBay is as simple as registering your name, or your business name. There are some details that you'll need to include in your registration as a seller, such as where you are located and how you plan on shipping your sold items.

Your goal as an eBay powerseller should be to look as professional as you can so that buyers take you seriously and learn to trust your reputation. Setting up an "online" shop is one way that you can gain a more professional outlook among the many sellers that can be found on eBay.

There are several different options available at eBay that will help you to make a good impression on buyers. You don't want buyers to think of you as just another eBay seller and pass you by for a more professional seller. When you first start selling your items on eBay you'll find that there is a learning curve as you find out what works for you and what doesn't. The important thing is to be flexible so that you can make changes to the way that you sell in your favor.

Seller Registration

All types of people and businesses are using eBay to sell their products. This includes the stay-at-home mom who is supplementing her family's income by selling craft products to large companies such as IBM who are seeing huge profits by selling online through eBay. When you sell items on eBay you can reach a large number of customers all around the world.

There are many benefits to selling on eBay. Some of these legal and financial benefits include:

- The low cost of registering at eBay.
- The ability to have fast and secure transactions with your buyers.
- Tax laws that are clearly defined.
- Accounting advice that even an amateur can follow.
- Low advertising costs.
- Free advertising tools.

There are many books that have been published that show you how successful you can be selling on eBay. This is a great market niche itself, to focus on the sale of items that show others how to sell, what to sell, and what to sell it for.

With so many benefits of selling on eBay more and more people are taking advantage of the opportunity. Make sure that you're one of the successful sellers by knowing all of the legal and financial angles of the eBay selling process. The sellers who fail are often the ones who remain blind to the legal side of selling online through eBay. Studies show that the most successful sellers on eBay operate businesses that are well organized and maintain perfect financial records of each and every transaction that they do both through eBay and with their wholesalers.

The first thing that you will have to do in order to sell on eBay to is register. There are several reasons why you first have to register on eBay. These include:

- EBay requires a certain amount of personal information from you. This is to keep the eBay site secure.
- EBay requires that you register with them before you can begin selling an item or bidding on other saleable items.
- Registration will provide you with updates on the latest eBay information and deals.

Registration at eBay is easy. All you have to do is follow the steps laid out for you. You will be required to provide your name, address, phone number, and a valid e-mail address. Many eBay powersellers choose to use a business name for their online transactions. You'll want to include this business name in your eBay registration.

The next step needed for registration is your online user ID. This is the ID by which you will be known as both a buyer and seller. Make sure to choose an ID name that sounds businesslike and professional. You will not want to come up with a cute name only to want to change it to something more sophisticated at a later date. Choose a password that is easy for you to remember.

Once you have completed the first two steps you simply have to check your e-mail for confirmation of your registration. You will then need to set up a seller's account. You will be asked to provide a valid credit or debit card as well as provide your banking information. This is necessary so that when you start selling your items eBay has accurate and legitimate information about how and where you will be accepting payment. EBay also needs your banking and credit information so that they can bill you appropriately for the small fees owed to them for any listing fees and commissions. Any personal information collected by eBay is done through a secure system so you do not have to worry about security issues.

The registration process takes only a few minutes for you to complete. Make sure your credit card and banking information is accurate and up to date to avoid confusion and error later.

During the registration process at eBay you'll be required to provide information about yourself and the items that you're selling. One of the things that you'll want to remember is to always keep the information in your seller profile current. Not only does eBay need to have this current information, sellers want to see that your information is accurate since it lends you a high degree of professionalism.

Your email address: When you first register with eBay you'll be need to use a current email address for the registration process. If you change your email address it's not necessary to register again. You want to maintain the status that you've built up as a successful seller on eBay by simply notifying eBay of your email address change. There is a "Change of Email Address" form that you can fill out and return to eBay that makes the change easy and fast. It's important that you don't register with your new email address because when you do you risk losing the information and data that correlates with your old email address. Should you mistakenly reregister with a new email address it can take eBay administration up to two weeks to merge the data from the old address to the new one. In the event that you do register again with a new email address you can contact eBay at ukemerge@ebay.com to let them know.

Your User ID: You can change your User ID at any time by using the "Change User ID" form. Your User ID is an important aspect of your eBay account. It's a way for buyers to identify you easily, especially when you're relying on repeat sales from the same buyers. You don't want to take the chance of buyers not finding you by changing your User ID. This is why it's important to create a User ID that you know is right for your business when your first register with eBay so that you avoid these changes. Your User ID should be a reflection of you and your business as opposed to a cute user name. Remember that buyers are going to identify you by this User ID so you want to be as professional as possible.

Your eBay password: Your password is your access to your eBay account so you'll want to remember it and protect it. If you want to change your password at any time you can use the "Change Password" form on the eBay website. There is also a "Forgot Your Password" form that you can fill out if you forget what your password is. You'll receive notification in your email of how you can change your password so that you can access your eBay seller's account. Your present password will stay valid until you change it, so if you forget your password you won't be able to access your account until you fill out the "Forgot Your Password" form and make the password change and respond back to eBay with replying email.

Your account information: When you want to make any other account changes that include information about your account or yourself, you can contact eBay by using the "Change Your Registered Information" form. This form will allow you to make any changes to your account that you need eBay and buyers to know. Keep in mind that any changes may take a day or two to be implemented on your account information page. Plan your changes accordingly so that you let your buyers see what you want them to see.

Other administration features: There are other administration features at eBay that you should be aware of so that you can become familiar and proficient with the selling process. The more experienced and comfortable you are moving around the eBay website the more you can focus on the selling of your products and the promotion of your business.

If you're looking for a certain feature of eBay, and can't seem to find it, don't hesitate to contact them by email to find the appropriate place where you need to look.
Some of the other administrative features that you can find on eBay include:

- Feedback Forum: The Feedback Forum is filled with information about your eBay transactions. This information is available for other eBay users to see.
- My eBay: This eBay feature allows you to view your current, and historical, selling and bidding information. This is handy feature to have since you can find out in one viewing what you've sold and what you've bidding on if you're buying something from another seller.
- About Me: The "About Me" feature of eBay lets you provide any other information to eBay registered users that you want them to know. This can include personal or business information.

EBay administrative services are there to make your selling experience as easy as possible and so that your business can succeed. Take advantage of these administrative services whenever you can so that you build a solid and positive relationship between eBay and yourself.

Listing Your Items

There are some simple basics that you should know about listing your items for sale on eBay. The more items that you list the more experienced you'll become in knowing how to write descriptions to entice buyers to take a longer look at the item that you're selling than the items of other sellers.

The first thing that you need to do is find items that you want to sell. For your first few selling attempts choose items that you yourself like so that you can create a listing that you can relate to. Find similar items that are for sale on eBay so that you get a good idea of how much the item is worth, what other sellers are selling it for, and what category it best fits into. To find items that are similar to the one that you're selling use the following steps:

- Use the "Search" button at the top of the eBay webpage.
- Select the "Advanced Search" and type in key search words.
- Choose the "Completed Items Only" option.

You'll quickly have a listing of items that were for sale on eBay but are now ended so that you can see what items are popular and what didn't sell.

Once you have your item ready to sell you're ready to begin listing it. The steps that you'll need to complete, in the following order, are:

- Select the format that you want to use to sell your item.
- Choose the best category for the item.
- Write a title that catches the eye of buyers.
- Write a complete description of the item making sure to include all the specifics such as measurements and condition.
- Include photos of the item that you're selling in the listing.
- Let buyers know where you live.
- Use some of the promotion tools available at eBay to promote the item.
- Include the payment that you'll accept for the item as well as information about shipping and packaging.

Be creative and step outside of the box. You need to establish new ways of marketing the items that you're selling. Take time to examine your competitors on eBay so that you know what they're doing and what you have to do better.

Once you are registered and have set up your seller's account you are ready to list the items that you want to sell. This is known as your eBay "listing". Your goal is to create a listing that is sensational and stands out from other listings. The secret to making money on eBay is to attract as many bidders as possible. There are several different sections that you can complete to create an eBay listing that is perfect for the item that you are selling. These include:

- Selecting a selling format that is right for you. Do you want to use the online auction format or set a definite fixed price for your items? You may want to experiment with several items and use a different selling format for each one. Keep track of which selling format works best for which items. The "Buy It Now" option may work wonderfully for one particular item but for another item it may be more advantageous to sell using the online auction format. Once you have experimented with a few items you will soon know what selling format to use for which of your sellable items.
- Choose the right category for your items. You will want to find the category or categories that best define the items you are selling. This is so that target buyers are able to easily and quickly find your item. If you are unsure about what category to choose for you items it is wise to play it safe and list them in more than one category.

- Write a descriptive title for your items. Choose words that define what you are selling and that will appear in any search that a buyer might try on eBay. Remember that you are competing with many other powersellers to get the attention of buyers and earn money. Your title is important because eBay's search engine works by reading the title line. You should try and use some key words in your title line for these search purposes. Identity the item clearly. If possible mention a brand name. The more information contained in your title line the more bidders you will attract to your listing.
- Description of your items. This is your opportunity to be creative and promote your item. A description should be written in some type of logical order. You should: (a) describe what the item is, (b) include the title, (c) include the artist, author or manufacturer of the item, (d) indicate identifying marks or other identifying information, (e) describe what the item is made of, (f) list the size and dimensions, (g) describe the condition of the item, and (h) include any special history or features that you think the buyer should know. It is also important to include one line in your description that encourages buyers to e-mail you with any questions.
- Use pictures. People like to see exactly what they are bidding on. EBay makes the process of including pictures in your listings an easy process. Pictures will attract buyers to your items. If you are posting more

than one photo use your most informative picture first, one that includes all the features of your item. Take the time to get the lighting in the photo right and the setup of the item correct so that you are taking a top-quality picture. Remember that a picture is worth a thousand words and will sell your item.
- Price. Decide what price you want to establish for the items you are selling. Determine whether you are using the online auction format or are using the "Buy It Now" option. You will also want to decide how long you want your listing to run. It is important to carefully determine what price is best for the item you are selling. Take the time to look at similar items that are selling on eBay. Research your competitors and see what they are doing. If you want to sell crystal vases, for example, you should take a look to see at what price other vases are being sold and at what prices they are listed. It is important that you research similar items so that you know what price to charge and if there is a market for what you want to sell. This step is vital since you may discover that you can't compete with current sellers on price or there is simply no market for what you have to offer.
- Indicate your payment and shipping preferences. You should offer as many payment options for the buyer as possible, including credit cards. The more payment options that you offer potential bidders the more

attention your item will attract. This will ensure you success as an eBay powerseller.

It is important to keep in mind that most buyers browse through the categories and items that interest them. Your eBay listing needs to be an attention-getter so that you give the buyer a reason to linger and take a longer look at the item that you are selling. Remember to check your spelling and avoid spelling mistakes. Misspelling of words is unprofessional and may make the difference between selling your item and having the listing expire without a sale.

Try to avoid using words in your eBay listing such as "rare" or "amazing". These are fluff words and will not convince buyers that they need your item just because it is amazing. Buyers will make their decision about the rarity of your item based on the concise and accurate information that you provide in you listing description.

When you are satisfied with the way the listing looks for your item you are ready to place the listing on eBay for buyers to bid on. Make sure to take a look at the way your listing looks online after you have completed the online steps. Make revisions to your listing if you're the least bit unsure about how it looks. It may take you a few tries for the first few items that you list but the effort will be well worth it.

EBay has administrative services that will help you create an item listing that give you the impact that you need to make those sales. In fact, eBay will write your item descriptions for you if you lack the confidence or the talent to do so yourself. You may want to take advantage of this administrative feature until you get the hang of being a powerseller on eBay.

Cost of listing: Selling on eBay costs you very little and this is one of the biggest appeals of this auction site. The cost of listing an item for sale on eBay will vary depending on the listing price of the item. This means that you can sell multiple items at a very low cost to you as an eBay powerseller.

If you decide to sell your items through an online shop you'll have to pay a bit more for the listing price but this also means that there will be more advantages to you as a seller. You'll be able to display all of the items that you have for sale at a lost cost that allows you to focus your business expenses in other areas, such as advertising or the purchase of products to sell. If you're going to be selling your items through an online shop the first 30 days will be free so that you can determine if this format is right for you and what you're selling.

Many buyers will take a look at all of the items that a seller has for sale. You want to make it as easy for the buyer as possible to find out all they can about what you're selling and who you are.

Writing Descriptions that Sell the Item

The title that you give your listings and the description that you provide are going to make all the difference when it comes to the sale of your products. The title and the description are your form of advertising in the eBay community. Without solid titles and strong descriptions you stand the chance of losing buyers to other sellers who stand out in the crowd. Your goal should be to become one of these sellers that stand out in that crowd.

Creating a strong title: Buyers at eBay will notice the product that you're selling from the title that you write for the item. You want to create a title that is immediately eye catching so that buyers want to linger for that crucial extra minute to read your description. Following are some guidelines for writing a strong, eye-catching title:

- Try to use words that are highly descriptive and that fully describe the item that you're selling.
- If appropriate include the key words in the title such as (1) brand names, (2) artist name, (3) designer names, or (4) any other identifying words that you know buyers will recognize.
- You need to precisely say what the item is. Don't be afraid to include the category name in the item title since it never hurts to emphasize this.

- Try to choose words in the title that buyers might use to search for items. This will bring more buyers to your item page.
- You only have so much space for a title so make the most of the words that you use. You don't want to use words that have no meaning, such as "incredible", which really tells the buyer nothing about the item that you're selling.
- Take a look at similar items that sold for a good price. See what titles those sellers used to encourage buyers to read through the description of the item that they were selling.
- There are some types of titles which eBay prohibits the use of. This includes titles that (1) use profane language, (2) use words the lead a buyer to believe the product is "illegal", (3) titles that include phone numbers, email addresses, or URLs, (4) titles that don't adequately describe the item that you're selling in any way.

When you follow these tips you'll be well on your way to creating titles that catch the eyes of buyers.

Creating a strong description: The more time that you put into writing a good description for the items that you're selling, the better chance you have of getting a lot of bids and selling at a high price. A description that is strong and filled with a lot of information will (1) give buyers all that they need to know to want to place a bid on your item, and (2) leave buyers with the impression that you care about what you're selling.

Sellers are always trying new techniques when it comes to item descriptions. Some of the more interesting things that you might want to include in the description are telling the buyer why you personally like the item that you're selling, letting the buyer know what appeals to you about the item, and what use the item might have to anyone who is considering placing a bid.

There are some things that you should include in the description of the products that you're selling. Some of this specific information should include:

- A clear explanation of what the item is.
- What the item is made of and the year that it was made.
- Who created the item, such as artist or author.
- What is the current condition of the item.
- What are the measurements of the item.
- Are there any distinguishing features of the item that the buyer should know about.
- What is the history of the item that you're selling.

There are obviously some pieces of information that you won't be able to include in the item description. Keep in mind that buyers have the ability to get in touch with you if they want to ask for more information.

There are some definite things that you should avoid when it comes to the description of the item. This includes:

- Never include any false information that will deceive a buyer.
- Avoid what is called "keyword spam". This means that you can't include keywords that aren't related to the item that you're selling, such as throwing in a brand name when you're not selling that particular brand.

Before you finalize your description make sure that you've included all the relevant information. Critical information that you should include:

- Information about your payment methods.
- Information about packaging and shipping.
- Where you're located.
- Any other information that can make the difference between a sale and a non-sale.

As a final note, make sure that check the spelling and grammar of your item descriptions before you submit. Nothing looks more unprofessional than an eBay listing that has spelling and grammar mistakes.

Including Photos in your EBay Listing

To achieve any degree of success as a seller on eBay you'll need to include a picture of the item that you're selling. Buyers are drawn to those listings that have a good, clear photo of the item.

When you're taking a picture of the item there are some basic guidelines that you should follow to make the most of this photo opportunity:

- Make sure that the lighting is good so that you get pictures that are clear and natural. If you're taking a picture outside make sure to use a flash if you need to increase the brightness of the picture.
- Use a backdrop of some kind for smaller items. Try to avoid using a white backdrop as this put too much contrast into the picture.
- Remove other objects from the picture that have no relevance to the item that you're selling.
- Get as close as you can without losing focus.
- Take pictures of sections of the item that you're selling so that buyers can see all sides.
- Take pictures of any distinguishing marks on the item, such as manufacturer stamps on the bottoms of vases.

After you've taken the picture eBay will walk you through the process of uploading the photo to your listing page. When you download the "EBay Picture Services Application" it will be easy for you to manage and upload all your pictures.

You want to develop a design for your online business that is going to enhance your business image and that will add strength to your Internet presence on eBay. This strategy is vital to the success of your business. Your goal should be to develop a design for your business that you can use in all areas of promoting your online website: advertising through your eBay description, creating strong titles, and including great pictures with your listings. You want to create a business design that will be remembered and recognized by your eBay customers, and that builds trust and reliability in your business as well as consistency.

The way you describe the items that you're selling can make all the difference between a sale or loosing a buyer to another seller. Take some time to learn what works when it comes to item descriptions as well as how you should be designing your listing.

The key to success at eBay is being familiar with the things that work. Most successful sellers have a wide variety of products to sell. They learn to manage their listings effectively and efficiently to make the most out of the quick minute which a buyer spends looking at your listing.

If you want your online business to profit and prosper then you need to become an expert when it comes to the publicity of the items that you have for sale on eBay. Publicity, or your eBay listing, can earn you a reputation as the expert in your target market, gain the trust and respect of eBay buyers', and in the end earn your business the profits that you need to succeed. Your goal should be to do all of the above without spending thousands of dollars on traditional, and often risky, methods of selling and advertising on the Internet.

EBay is a great online location for you to sell the items that you want to earn money to supplement your income or quit your job and sell at eBay at a full time level.

Rules for Selling

There are several rules that you should be aware of so that you don't make any crucial mistakes when it comes to selling your items on eBay. Although the process of selling on eBay is as simple as possible there are still some things that you should know before you start selling and growing your business.

One of the most important things that you need to be aware of is keeping your selling and buying transactions as safe and secure as possible. There are policies in place which ensure the safety and privacy of the financial information of the people who are buying from you as well as your own financial information. Some of the other things that you'll need to know when you sell on eBay include:

- EBay's tax policy and regulations.
- The policies for listing at eBay.
- How to sell your items internationally.

Tax policy: When you sell on eBay you need make sure that you observe all of the taxes that are applicable to the sale. This includes domestic tax laws, international tax laws, any local statutes, and any ordinances. When you sell on eBay you are committing the act of listing, soliciting, and selling certain items. These items and the selling practice are liable to fees and taxes.

Policy violations: There are some types of polices that are not allowed on eBay. It's important that you are aware of these polices so that you don't find yourself in violation of the rules. The last thing that you want is to face a temporary suspension because you weren't aware of a certain policy. These violations include:

- Shill bidding is not allowed on eBay.
- You may not solicit your items off the eBay website while you are soliciting them on eBay.
- You can not, on your own, interrupt a transaction that is already in process.

If buyers, or other sellers, find that you are in violation of any of the rules and regulations that eBay clearly outlines they can file what is called a "trading offence" with eBay administration. As well, if you find that any other sellers are in violation of these policies you can file an offence.

Trading offence: If you want to file a trading offence against another seller you need to follow this procedure:

- Read once again the policy page at eBay which clearly outlines the policies that must be followed. Make sure that the eBay user is in violation of one of these policies. There is a link on this webpage which you can use to send a report directly to eBay.
- Fill in the report with all the required information that eBay will need to make a decision about the trading offence. This report information should include any emails that are connected with the offence, as well as subject lines that are clear and easy to understand.
- Only file a trading offence report once. The more times that you report an offence the slower the process will move as eBay administrators need to read each report and add it to the file.

EBay will investigate all trading offence that are filed and will make a decision based on the circumstances. Some of the actions that eBay may take to deal with trading offences are a warning, a temporary suspension, or a permanent suspension.

EBay Store Fronts

EBay Store Fronts are another way that you can sell items on eBay. The products that you choose to sell will have a front row seat to eBay buyers who are looking for the items that you're offering.

EBay is one advertising opportunity that you might not want to miss so that you can maximize your business exposure on the Internet. When you use an eBay Store Front you can connect with thousands of people every day who shop on eBay.

It costs very little for you to open an eBay Store. For just a low cost each month you can start to boost your Internet presence, increase your sales, and add to your customer database. When you start an eBay Store you'll have these tools at your disposal:

- An online Store Front that is completely yours to develop and create to fit your business needs.
- Tracking methods and a way to analyze how your business is doing within the eBay community.
- Easy tools to manage the running of your eBay Store.
- Tools at hand for marketing and merchandising your product.

There are many benefits of an eBay Store Front. When you open an eBay Store Front you'll find that there are many benefits to you and your business. An eBay Store Front gives you the opportunity to reach thousands of people each day and increase the exposure that you need to obtain more customers. One of the big benefits of having an eBay Store Front is that it gives your website a look of professionalism that is going to give you the credibility that you need to reach customers that are looking for a particular product or service on the Internet. It takes only a few minutes to start your eBay store, which means that you'll be up and running in no time, and ready for customers to find you.

You'll be able to customize your Store Front to the exact design that you feel best stylizes the products that you're selling. There are over 20 different design categories that you can choose from when you sign up with eBay Store Front. And you'll be able to have a unique address on the Internet for your Store Front so that customers can find you fast and easily, book marking your Store Front website so that they can return again later for repeat sales and to find out what's new in your Store.

Each month you'll have access to a variety of reports that will let you know exactly how you're doing. Some of the data information that you'll receive each month includes:

- Traffic report: traffic reports so that you know how many web visitors are stopping by your eBay Store Front.
- Sales report: sales reports, to let you know how many sales your Store Front has generated.
- Accounting information: accounting information that you can use to export your PayPal and eBay sales transactions into accounting software programs such as QuickBooks or your own Excel spreadsheet.

When it comes to the promotion of your eBay Store Front you won't be left in the cold, since eBay will give you all the help that you need to bring customers to your eBay

Store. EBay will list your Store Front on all the appropriate listings within their website pages as well as send out marketing correspondence to your customers.

When you sign up with eBay Store Front you'll have a search engine in the content of your store. This means that your customers will be able to use this search tool to find the products, or services, that you're selling.

You'll save a lot of time using the eBay Store Front to sell your products and spend more time concentrating on your business and other marketing strategies. When you sign up with eBay Store Front you'll see a definite increase in your sales and profits, as well as watch your customer database grow and turn into repeat sales.

EBay Administrative Services

There are several different administrative services that have been put into place to give you as much success at eBay as possible. When you first start selling your items on eBay you may find that, even though the process is very simple, there are still many things that you need to learn. If your goal is to become an eBay powerseller you'll want to take the help that you can get so that you can learn all the ins and outs of the selling process.

Some of the administrative services that eBay provides include:

- Forums that help you promote and advertise the items that you're selling.

- Tips and techniques on how to improve your seller reputation.
- Help in managing and maintaining your item listings.
- Determining what payment options are best for you and your eBay business so that you make sure that you get paid.
- Determining what shipping options are best for you and your buyers.

When you first register at eBay you'll want to take some time to familiarize yourself with all of the services that are available to you as a seller. Make sure that you know where to go when you have questions about payment and shipping options before any problems arise. You want to be as prepared as possible before you make your first eBay sale.

Keep in mind that eBay is always changing and improving their website and services. This means that you need to pay attention to announcements so that you stay on top of the latest advancements. As an eBay powerseller you'll want to understand all the latest policy changes so that you're not caught unaware.

What Sells and What Doesn't Sell

EBay listings include all kinds of items for sale, from the plain and ordinary to the wild and amazing. You will have to determine what types of items you want to sell. There are some things you may want to consider before you make your decision. Are you going to be selling items that you already have around your home? Or are you going to find products in your local area that you are going to purchase with the intent of reselling the item and making a profit?

To give you an idea of what is being sold at eBay here are a few of the items offered for sale today:

- Collectibles: There are a wide range of collectibles that are sold every day on eBay. From the traditional fare of stamps, coins, and comic books to the more specialized items such as Beanie Babies™, Zippo™ lighters, and PEZ™ dispensers, eBay is by far the number one place on the Web to find the widest range of both popular and hard-to-find collectable items.
- Electronics: EBay is an excellent source to sell both new and used electronic items. Whether you are selling individual items or lots that have been purchased in bulk, there are always buyers for electronic goods of all shapes and sizes. Cell phones, stereo equipment, computers, and video games are just a few of the millions of high tech gadgetry that can be found across many sections of the eBay community.
- Antiques: Items in this category include everything from Asian vases to antique maps. If you are considering selling an antique make sure you know the value of the item so that you can verify the item's worth. If you have any documentation that legitimizes

the age and antique value of the item you should make note of this in your item listing. Take a photo of any documentation that supports the value and age of the antique you are selling. You should also take a picture of any identifying marks on the antique to establish its worth. The more information you can provide potential buyers the more successful you will be with the sale.

- Books: Books are a very popular sale item on eBay. Sub-categories include children's books, poetry, reference books, and the latest fiction. If you are thinking about selling books at eBay you will have to do your research very carefully to make certain that you are selling at a competitive market value. One of the best things about selling books is that they are easy to package and ship to the seller. Books are relatively difficult to damage during mailing and shipping costs will be minimal compared to the shipping expenses of larger, more fragile items bought on eBay. You will want to find out the availability of a certain book you are thinking about selling. If the book is readily available through other selling markets, such as bookstores and supermarkets, there may not be a high demand for the book and you may want to reconsider spending time listing it on eBay. Make sure the books you are selling are in good condition. If there is wear and tear or damage to the book be sure to make mention of this in your eBay listing. You want to give the buyer as much information as possible.

- DVDs and Movies: DVDs and movies are a great item to sell on eBay. Be sure to include information such as media format (DVD/VHS/Beta/Laserdisc/etc) and encoding information (such as PAL/NTSC). When dealing with box sets, be sure to include bonus items and packaging details.
- Arts and Crafts: On eBay you will find many examples of the modern "cottage industry" with individuals and small "mom and pop" operations who create arts and crafts of every flavor imaginable. From homemade candles to home fired ceramics to hand strung beads and artwork, eBay has no shortage of merchandise that caters to those who desire items with that "personal touch". In addition to offering the final products of many creative individuals, eBay also hosts many vendors of arts and crafts supplies.

There are some items that you are prohibited to sell on eBay. EBay will end your listing if you violate their policy of what you can not sell. As well as items that you are prohibited from selling, some items may be considered questionable (can only be listed under certain conditions) or potentially infringing (item may be in violation of certain copyrights). There are some of the items that you are prohibited from selling on eBay:

- Alcohol

- Counterfeit items
- Firearms, Ammunition, Replicas, and Militaria
- Drugs and drug paraphernalia
- Plants and seeds
- Stocks and other securities
- Lottery tickets
- Stolen property

The list of items to sell on eBay is endless. If you do your research well you will be able to make an informative decision about what you are going to sell on eBay to make money. Experiment with different items to see what you enjoy selling and at which you are most successful.

Finding Items to Sell

There are many places for powersellers to find items to sell, and make a profit from, on eBay. With a little bit of research and as little as 4 or 5 hours a week, you too can find yourself running a successful e-business using eBay as your marketing vehicle and e-commerce engine. Here are some suggestions for where to begin searching for merchandise for sale on eBay which can result in the highest profit margins and therefore more money in YOUR pocket:

- Flea markets. It is possible to find many hidden treasures at flea markets in your local area. It is common for attics to be cleared out and surplus stock from a variety of retail outlets to be emptied into the flea market ecosystem in the hopes of making at least some amount of money from what is considered to be "surplus" or "salvaged". It is here that you can find the best deals, but you can also uncover hard-to-find collectables, electronics, and many other categories of merchandise that are ripe for the picking for resale on eBay. Another thing to look out for when scouring flea markets is geographically-specific items. Items which may be hard to find in one part of the world may be very easy to find in another. Due to the fact that eBay is a global market, it can pay off very well to keep your eyes peeled for these little nuggets of profit.

- EBay itself. Another great place to find the types of things to resell on eBay is right there on eBay. Although at first thought it may seem a little counterproductive, what it all really boils down to is getting a good deal at a good time. Try to focus on types of merchandise you have more than a cursory knowledge of. For example, if you are a comic book buff who has been collecting for years, you will have a great eye for that particular subsection of eBay (and a much greater chance of knowing a good deal when you see it). Of particular focus should be auctioneers letting go of entire lots of merchandise for events like estate sales, unclaimed freight, or store closings.

Digging through eBay's mountain of merchandise when you know what you are doing can prove not only profitable, but a lot of fun as well.

- Swap meets/conventions. It can also pay to take note when your local area is hosting special interest conventions and swap meets, such as gun shows, comic book conventions and the like. With a little research on eBay regarding the current market for the particular classes of merchandise focused on at these meets, studious, and diligent individuals can profit greatly from very little initial investment. In addition to the diverse collections of various types of items that these meets and conventions will place at your fingertips, you can also usually acquire a lot of freebies (or schwag, in convention nomenclature), which can be easily resold to enthusiasts of the particular subject you are participating in the meet for.
- Buying in bulk. This is less of a "where" and more of a "how", but it's definitely applicable: It seems like a lot of powersellers find something they get a good bargain on locally and sell it to a wide market that doesn't have that same access. For instance, you might discover that computer desk shelves are selling on eBay for quite a bit more than your local bulk retailer charges. This is an excellent opportunity for you to profit from your location and what you have access to. To take this another step further you may wish to contact the manufacturer and find a wholesaler to purchase it in bulk. Some manufacturers will work with you in this way and some won't, you'll just have to experiment and find out. Another good idea is visiting closeout

stores and outlets. It's a pot luck selection that sells for way below catalogue price, and eBay sellers are looking to make the profit margin from people who don't have access to these stores.

- Clearance racks at malls. Try searching the clearance racks in your local shopping malls for great deals on clothing. Many people live in areas that are not serviced by shopping malls and therefore don't have access to the types of merchandise that you do. It's a good idea to visit these stores during big sales, especially right after the holiday period or at the turn of seasons when retailers will be trying to get rid of their old stock to make room for the new. Particularly focus on trendy stores that deal in expensive brand name items. Often you will be able to find very popular, trendy labels for a fraction of their retail cost, sometimes even below cost.

- Garage Sales. Don't forget to check your local paper for garage/lawn sales. Usually you can find great deals if you are willing to dig and sift through a few garage sales every weekend.

- Your own attic. You would be shocked what some people, and maybe even YOU, have in the attic. The next time you do some spring cleaning, be sure to take the time to dig through some of those boxes, wooden chests, and foot lockers collecting dust in your attic, basement or storage shed. Anything from antiques to unique collectables can be found by just digging around bit a rainy April afternoon.

Finding a Wholesaler

If you want to have a profitable online business selling products on eBay you'll need have a constant source of items to sell. Rather than finding items to sell at garage sales and flea markets you'll want to establish relationships with wholesalers who are selling items that you're interested in selling. There are several ways that you can find the right wholesaler for you:

- Wholesale lots: You can find wholesale lots on the eBay website so that almost all the searching for products is done for you. There are many categories that are listed featuring almost any type of product imaginable. This includes electronics, books, collectibles, music, clothing, and household items.
  Take some time to do your own buyer search on eBay to find out what items that are listed are popular. Then you can focus on a similar product so that you can sell at competitive prices. When you find a wholesale product that you want to sell you can sell it for a considerable profit on eBay. The important thing to do is thoroughly research the market on eBay before you decide on what products to sell.

- Storage unit auctions: Another great way to find products to sell on eBay is by finding out when storage unit businesses are having an auction. Most storage unit businesses will auction several times each year to get rid of unwanted items that have been unclaimed for a certain period of time. This is a great way for you pick up some cheap items that you can resell for a great profit. The items that you know won't sell on eBay can be given away to charity or you can hold your own garage sale to make a penny or two.
- Search the Internet: The Internet is a great way to find wholesalers that have some great products for you to sell online at eBay. Type a keyword such as wholesaler, liquidator, or wholesale trading into any search engine and you'll be rewarded with a huge listing of wholesalers from around the world.
- Wholesale directories: You can find wholesalers by looking in a wholesale directory. You can find a directory on the Internet. You'll be able to find lists of distributors, manufacturers, and wholesalers in well formatted categories that make it easy for you to find what you're looking for.
- Exporters and importers: If you're looking at the big picture, and plan on selling a wide variety of items on eBay, you may want to contact those companies that specialize in imports from overseas.

- Local wholesalers: Look for wholesalers where you live since there are usually many sources available locally. You want to find one or more wholesalers from who you can purchase the items that you know you can sell on eBay. A local wholesaler will save you money on shipping costs and you'll be able to supplement your inventory at any time without the wait of shipping.

When you're looking for a wholesaler it's important to find one or more that specialize in the products that you're interested in. If you've done your research on eBay you should already know which items are current hot sales and which ones aren't. Another thing to remember when you're looking for a wholesaler is that the fewer people are already buying from the wholesaler the more unique your product will be when you sell it on eBay. Take some time to find products that are one of a kind, such as a craft item that is rare to find.

Building a Powerseller Reputation

The absolute most critical element to the eBay selling experience is building your eBay powerseller reputation. The basic component of the reputation system on eBay is user feedback. For every eBay transaction, including auctions and "Buy it now" transactions, both parties involved in the deal will have an opportunity to assign a positive, neutral, or negative score to their transaction, as well as provide textual comments. Here's how eBay describes the feedback system on their website:

> "Every eBay user has a feedback score based on ratings from other members. Feedback lets you reward eBay users and inform the community about your experiences with others. Typically, members give a positive rating if they are happy with a transaction and a negative when basic obligations have not been met. Keep in mind that what you say about other members becomes a permanent part of their eBay reputation."

In order to be successful in any capacity on eBay, whether you are buying or selling, it will be necessary to develop a positive powerseller reputation within the eBay community by embodying sound business practices and good customer relations. Here are a few suggestions to get you started:

- Keep clear and open channels of communication with your customers. Make sure you answer questions from potential bidders in a timely manner and be particularly mindful to field any inquiries from auction winners. Being quick to respond to perceived problems can mean the difference between a positive and a negative feedback which can and will be a direct influence on potential buyers out there.

- Participate in as many transactions as possible. Besides your feedback ratio, potential buyers will also give some scrutiny to the sheer volume of business you do. If given the choice of doing business with two individual sellers, and one of those sellers has a tried and true reputation with thousands of transactions, the buyer is most likely going to go with the seller that has the most experience. That seller should be you.
- Be open and honest. Being the most communicative powerseller on eBay is no good if you are being misleading or dishonest with your customers. It is imperative that you take every step possible to ensure that you're being as honest as you can be with your clientele. If you are selling an item that may have perceivable flaws, it is a good idea to make sure that that is clear in the item summary. Be sure to be up front regarding your shipping costs and any other fees that may be incurred above and beyond the winning bid on the item. Never participate in questionable, sneaky practices such as profiting from shipping costs by padding the final shipping and handling price. While trickery like that may make you a little extra in the short term, you will end up paying for it in negative feedback and/or bad word-of-mouth from dissatisfied customers.

Selling Techniques

There are many things you can do to increase the sale of your items on eBay. Not only do you need to register on eBay and create a seller's account, you need to use all the techniques and tips at your fingertips to see consistent and increased sales. Here are some general techniques for you to consider, some of which have been touched on in other chapters as well as here:

- Treat your buyer's right. It is very important to build up a good relationship with your buyers and potential buyers. Be sure to answer all e-mail questions as well as you can. Make sure that you leave positive feedback for buyers. This is an important step towards building up your reputation as a powerseller on eBay.
- Do not expect "instant wealth". If you start selling with the intent of becoming rich instantly you may be disappointed to find that earning a substantial profit selling on eBay takes some time and effort. You need to build up your eBay business over a period of several months. If you are consistent and determined you will quickly see the results in your bank account.
- Remember that selling on eBay is a business. If you keep that in mind you will treat it with more seriousness.
- Learn how to stand out from the crowd of other sellers on eBay.

- Offer as many payment options as possible, including credit cards. The more payment options you offer prospective buyers, the more bidders your product will attract and the more successful your selling on eBay will be.
- Be knowledgeable about your shipping options. Offer as many options as you can, especially for international buyers. Be VERY clear when outlining your shipping policies for bidders.
- Be sure to write very descriptive listings for your merchandise. As much care should be taken in articulating the sale in words as there is to the photograph of your item.
- Constantly check out what the competition is doing. Make time to see what your competitors are selling and at what prices. You need to remain up-to-date so that you can remain competitive.
- Participate in the eBay online community areas. This includes the message boards and chat areas.
- Include measurements for any merchandise in which the dimensions or weight can be an issue.
- If you are going to be selling a LOT of items, consider opening an EBay store.
- Maintain a professional attitude. As with any other sector of the business world, a good professional attitude and a professional reputation will take you far.
- Keep track of all your sales records for tax purposes.

- Keep a database of your customers. Make sure you record business-critical information such as shipping address and contact information.

Finances: Try to keep your personal and business financial accounts as separate as possible. You want to have accurate records of your spending and profits from your eBay business without having them cross over to the other. You'll need to record all of your expenses and your income when they happen rather than when the cash leaves or comes into your hand. This type of an accounting system is called "accrual" accounting and is much more accurate than "cash" accounting where the transactions are only recorded when the cash actually changes hands between you and the buyer or you and the wholesaler.

You need to be honest about the changes in your income level. It's your legal responsibility to record any increase in income on your taxes.

It will be your responsibility to record and report the taxes that you owe. EBay won't accept any of the blame for any taxes that you fail to record and pay.

Permits and licenses: You'll need to contact a Customs and Excise office to register your new business and apply for an export permit if you're going to be selling your products internationally.

You'll also need to apply for a license to sell food products on the Internet. Make sure that you find out about all the permits and licenses you need in the area where you live to make sure that you have everything that you need to legally sell on eBay.

It's important that you accurately describe what it is that you're selling so that you don't misrepresent the item.

Selling Issues to Avoid

Of course, in dealing with online auctions there are many things you can do to improve your business. But in addition to all of the things you can do to make business better, there are also things that you should NOT do if you want to be a powerseller on eBay. There are some things that will gain you no benefit and can even HURT your business on eBay. Here is a short list of what NOT to do:

- Don't use music, big gaudy graphics, or other animations or a multicolored background in your listing.
- Don't rush to leave negative feedback for a non-paying bidder.
- Don't delay in shipping your items.
- Don't try to make a profit off of "handling charges".
- Don't use "As is" as a description in your listings.
- Don't wait for the buyer to leave feedback first.
- Don't fail to identify defects in your merchandise.
- Don't list your auctions so they end on a Holiday.
- Don't be afraid to accept international buyers.
- Don't make threats or use a negative tone in your listing.

Toolkits for EBay

There are many software tools out there that can help you make the most out of the eBay experience. From sniping software to data analysis to auction tools, you will find many useful utilities exist on the web to make your powerselling auctions more efficient and effective. Here are some examples of software you will find useful:

- Baycheck is a utility that allows quick access to a TON of user information. Using Baycheck, everything you need to know about a user is just a click away, like: Seller history, bidder history, feedback received, and feedback left.
- DeepAnalysis is eBay research software. Using DeepAnalysis eBay users can extract and analyze licensed eBay data and statistics for any eBay market sector, then use DeepAnalysis to reveal market trends and develop eBay strategies that will help you make money on eBay.
- Turbo Sniper provides: Auction sniping, standalone and server-based auction tracking, email automation, bulk search and data extraction, and universal automation and analysis.
- Bidnapper is another sniping tool.
- AuctionSleuth is combination sniping and buy-it-now bidding software that can help you find good deals on eBay.

EBay Pitfalls

Doing business on eBay isn't without its concerns and pitfalls. EBay is like any other business and is prone to fine details that need to be adhered to by anyone who wants to be a powerseller.

Sniping is one issue that many powersellers need to be aware of. Sniping is used by many buyers when they want to ensure that they are going to get the items that they want. Sniping allows these buyers to wait until the very before they place their bid on your item for sale. Most times this means that any buyer who really wants to buy what you're selling loses out on the opportunity since they don't have a chance to re-bid before your item listing expires. You can often recognize when your item has been bought by a buyer who is using a sniping technique: you'll notice that there is a last minute bid before your sale closes.

Sniping can have both a positive and a negative effect on you as a powerseller. In the positive light, sniping shows that what you're selling is in high demand. However, this also means that many items that you have for sale are being bought up by what are often other sellers on eBay, this giving "real" buyer's very little chance to make a purchase.

Another concern of dealing with eBay is the question of reliability. Many people ask themselves whether or not it's safe to do business on eBay either as a powerseller or as a buyer. No one wants to be deal with dishonesty where there is money and product changing hands. One thing that you need to be aware of as a powerseller is that eBay relies on the positive and negative feedback of buyers and sellers to make things work. How else are you going to know that a certain buyer has a good reputation and will pay you what you're owed? As a powerseller you can post feedback for a buyer that is positive, negative, or neutral. You can also leave comments about the transaction that will be helpful to other sellers in the future. With time, and the leaving of feedback, dishonest buyers will soon be identified. When a buyer or seller has too many negative feedbacks they are brought to the attention of eBay administration and they may have their privileges at eBay revoked so that they are prevented from doing further business. In some cases this information is turned over to law enforcement for further action.

User Agreement

As of 21 December 2004 there is a User Agreement in place at eBay for all registered users. The legal issues of the User Agreement have been put into place for your benefit and the benefit of eBay.

Some of the main points of the User Agreement are as follows:

- Eligibility of membership: EBay only allows membership to people who are 18 years or older. Buyers or sellers under the age of 18 must be under the legal supervision of someone over 18.

- User ID: All buyers and sellers will be required to have a User ID which they create at the time of their registration. You will be legally responsible for any type of action or transaction that takes place with the use of your User ID. It's important that you don't share your User ID with anyone else or that you sell it since you are the one who will be responsible if anything happens.
- Fees at eBay: You will be required to pay all of the fees that you owe to eBay on time. If you don't pay your fees you will face a temporary or permanent suspension from the eBay website. You will also be responsible for any taxes that are associated with the sale of your items.
- Personal information: Your personal information will remain the property and responsibility of eBay and will not be sold or mined to others. This means that you can be assured that any personal and financial information that you provide to eBay will remain private. The exception to this policy is if you are involved in illegal activities at which time your information will become accessible by legal authorities.
- Disputes: Any dispute that occurs between you and eBay should be immediately reported to "EBay Customer Support". After a fair investigation a decision will be made in due time.

Unauthorized Copyright

EBay has a policy in place that prohibits infringement of copyright laws. This policy is called the "anti-circumvention" policy. This policy makes it illegal for you to list or sell any items, such as software, hardware products or books, which will allow buyers of these items to make unauthorized copies of the following media or learn how to do so:

- Software programs
- DVDs
- CDs
- Books
- Video games

If any sellers are in violation of this policy the listing sale will be closed early and the seller may have their eBay account suspended if they are found to be in violation of the anti-circumvention policy more than once.

Bootleg copies of media are also prohibited under the anti-circumvention policy. If you're selling media, and you're unsure of the source, you should check out the background of the product before hand so that you don't find out later that you are in violation of the policy.

Conclusion

You are now ready to begin earning money by becoming a powerseller on eBay! The advice, suggestions, tools, and techniques presented to you in these chapters will have prepared you for what to expect when selling at eBay.

EBay will guide you through the process of becoming an online powerseller. Their website is packed with help and will answer any other questions you have about selling on eBay. Make sure to take advantage of their help section.

In this day and age we are all looking for ways to supplement our income so that we can save a little money for something special or to help pay our bills and debts. By selling on eBay you can earn that money without giving up your other job. You can work in the comfort of your own home so you don't have to worry about travel costs. You can spend time with your family while still earning money.

It won't take long before you start to see a substantial increase in the sale of your items when you follow the information that is outlined in this book. Whether you are selling items you already have in your home or whether you are buying items specifically for the purpose of resale, eBay provides you with the virtual Internet space to connect with buyers from all walks of life.

After reading this book you will have an edge over other sellers and will have the knowledge to build a successful Internet business for yourself. You will soon find yourself reaping the rewards and benefits that come from being an eBay powerseller!

We hope you have found this e-book useful. If you do your research carefully and keep organized, there is no limit to the money you can make selling on eBay. Sometimes it can be a little difficult to get started, but persistence and discipline will pay off in the end. There are all sorts of great reasons to start making money from selling on eBay today. Besides the potential to make a lot of profit, you will get to make your own hours and generally be your own boss, which is great. So give it a try today, you'll be glad you did.

www.ingramcontent.com/pod-product-compliance
Lightning Source LLC
Chambersburg PA
CBHW030955240526
45463CB00016B/2728